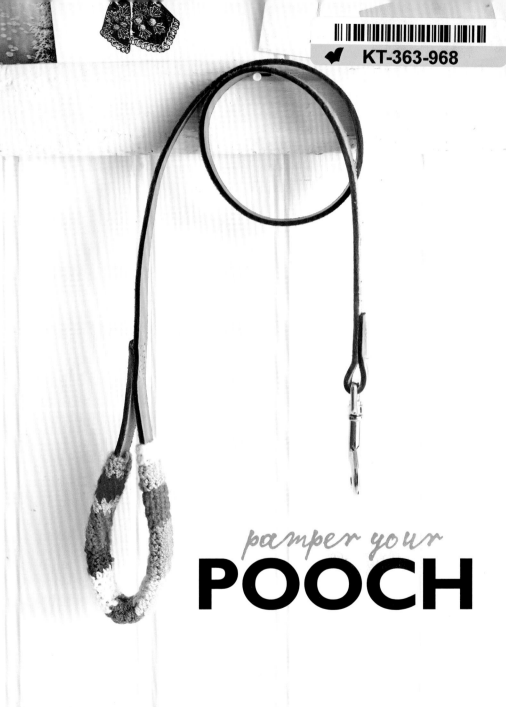

pamper your
POOCH

pamper your POOCH

30 practical presents for dogs

Rachelle Blondel

KYLE BOOKS

contents

introduction

From the moment their little wet nose arrives on the door-step a dog becomes part and parcel of the everyday goings on in your household. There to welcome you home with an eager wagging tail and eyes just sparkling love, to perch on your lap when you are feeling a little less than tip top, a dog's heart has no limits and will love you for every second of every day, even if you are cross with them for chewing the back door frame. So why not whip up a whole host of crafty bits and bobs to show your dog how cherished they are?

As you flick through the pages of this book, all manner of crafty projects to crochet, knit, sew and bake will catch your eye. Each and every one offers a most lovely but practical item to show your pooch that they are loved and cared for in every way. Plus they enable you to personalise your doggy paraphernalia to mix and match in with your own decorating style rather than having to settle for the everyday mundane doggy stuff, which too often comes along in various shades of brown.

Why not make them a warm cosy bed to snuggle into during those long hours of sleep that are essential for snoring the day away, topped with a knitted blanket for that burying, nose scruffing action that all dogs like to partake in every now and again? Keep them warm on your daily walk when the days turn wet and nippy with a made-to-measure dog coat. And when those sunny days show their smiles, tog them out with a jaunty neck scarf or most dapper bow tie for their saunter around the neighbourhood.

We are all thoughtful of where our food comes from nowadays and what indeed it is made from. If you whip up a few dog treats using ingredients from your kitchen cupboard you will know exactly what your dog is munching on and that it is keeping them healthy and bright.

Everything you make for your dog not only gives you the joy
of crafting your day away but also shows them how special
they are as proud owners of an array of handmade goodness
which in turn will be chewed, rummaged in, chased about and
proudly worn, all with a wagging tail and a thankful heart….

It seems fitting at this point to say a huge thank you to all the
dogs that have wandered my path with me. Each and every
one of you has brought a little bit of sunshine. I will always
have a dog by my side because without them days are dull and
not quite as shiny.

eat

Tasty, wholesome and easy-to-make treats. Whip up a batch or two, so you know exactly what is going in your dog's tum. Treats ideal to use for training, a munch to say I love you and even a birthday cake to celebrate your pooch's special day.

Everyone loves a cake on their birthday so why not indulge your dog with a little treat on theirs? Banana and honey cakes baked individually so your pooch doesn't over-do it are a delectable treat when topped with a delicious cream cheese and peanut butter frosting. Go to town with sprinkles and doggie choc drops and make your dog's day extra special.

doggie birthday cake

YOU WILL NEED

2 bananas

2 tablespoons rapeseed oil

1 egg, lightly beaten

3 tablespoons natural yogurt

1 tablespoon honey

200g wholewheat flour

1 teaspoon bicarbonate of soda

TOPPING FOR 1 CAKE

1 tablespoon cream cheese

1 tablespoon peanut butter

doggie chocolate buttons*

sprinkles

flags

MAKES 6 MUFFIN-SIZED CAKES

1 Preheat the oven to 180°C/gas mark 4.

2 Mash the bananas and mix with the oil, egg, yogurt and honey in a large bowl until everything is well combined.

3 Stir in the flour and bicarbonate of soda, then spoon into a muffin tin and bake for 15 minutes. Allow to cool.

4 Beat the cream cheese and peanut butter together and then swirl, pipe or spoon onto the top of the muffin.

5 Adorn with choc buttons, sprinkles and a flag or two and wish your doggie a very merry birthday.

Remaining cakes can be frozen without frosting for up to 3 months.

*Please do not use normal chocolate as it can be extremely harmful for your dog.

A birthday is not indeed a birthday without cake... even for dogs

We all need a cool-down treat during the hot days of summer and this includes our four-legged friends; with their furry coats they find it hard to keep cool on days when the temperature soars. These yummy frozen snacks will keep your hound chilled and entertained for a while and are quick and easy to prepare.

doggie pops

YOU WILL NEED

1 banana, sliced
1 apple, cored and chopped
5–6 strawberries
a handful of mint leaves
200ml natural yogurt
a spoonful of flaxseed oil, optional
mini bones or chew sticks, optional

MAKES 24

1 Place the fruit, mint, yogurt and flax seed oil, if using, in a blender and blitz until creamy and smooth.

2 Pour into silicon mini muffin tins, or any other suitable container – small yogurt pots sat on a tray are ideal – and place upright in the freezer.

3 After about 30 minutes check to see if they are starting to firm up and then (if using) pop a bone or chew in each one. If the pops aren't frozen enough to support the bone leave them to freeze for a while longer.

4 Leave overnight, then remove the pops from the container and place in a freezer bag for easier storage.

All dogs love treats and especially ones they can chew. Sweet potatoes are a great source of dietary fibre for your dog, along with vitamin B6, vitamin C, beta carotene and manganese. These chewy strips are simple to make and will soon become a firm favourite.

Stored in a sealed jar somewhere cool they will keep for a week.

sweet potato chew strips

I large sweet potato

MAKES 12–15

1 Turn your oven onto the lowest setting.

2 Slice the potato into thin strips and spread over a baking tray lined with baking parchment. Bake for 30 minutes. Turn the strips over, then bake for a further 30 minutes.

3 If, after this, there are still any soft areas, turn and bake again until they have firmed up.

4 Allow the strips to cool completely before storing in an airtight container.

Bake some wholesome goodness for your pooch by making these homemade dog biscuits. Made with carrots, coconut and peanut butter they will be loved by your dog and you can be assured they are getting a healthy, natural treat too.

dog biscuits

YOU WILL NEED

3 carrots, peeled and roughly chopped

150g oats

1 tablespoon coconut oil

1 tablespoon peanut butter

2 eggs

a spoonful chia or flax seeds, optional

MAKES 15–20

1 Preheat the oven to 180°C/gas mark 4 and line a large baking tray with baking parchment.

2 Place the carrots and oats in a food processer and blend until both are finely chopped.

3 Add the coconut oil, peanut butter and eggs and blend again, then empty the mixture into a bowl and chill for 30 minutes.

4 Place teaspoons of the mixture onto the baking tray and carefully flatten with a spoon. Place in the oven and bake for 20 minutes.

5 Place on a rack to cool and then store in an airtight container for up to one week.

doggie treats tin

Just to make sure there is no doubt who those delicious looking homemade treats belong to, it is advisable to store them in their very own 'treat tin' so there is no confusion when snacking late at night. Reuse dog food tins to make these useful little storage pots that will look good sitting on the Handy Wall Shelf (see page 42), which you must indeed make to keep everything dog related neat and tidy.

1 Begin by thoroughly cleaning the food tins, paying extra attention to the inside.

2 Sand any sharp edges on the inside of the tin.

3 Place the tins on a covered surface, preferably outside, and spray them with at least two coats of paint (follow the manufacturer's specific instructions). Leave the tins to dry for at least 24 hours longer if possible.

4 Glue the toy dogs to the lids. Allow the glue to set and completely cure before using (follow manufacturer's guidelines for curing times).

5 Using a strip of brown paper as a label, write or stamp the contents or some other jolly title onto the paper so that you can remember what's inside each tin. Fill with various treats and doggie bits.

YOU WILL NEED

food tins in various sizes
fine sandpaper
spray paint
strong glue
plastic toy dogs
food cover lids
brown paper, alphabet stamps and ink

If you're always in search of the perfect dog bowl, one that doesn't spill its contents as dinner is scoffed, then give this one a try. Using enamel pudding bowls will ensure dinnertime is a far more civilized affair with no chance of a broken bowl after a munching argy-bargy. The fact that they are often picked up for pence at charity shops and are pretty unbreakable makes them a great choice of food vessel. Adding a nifty blackboard square means you can chalk in your dog's name to make the bowl their very own.

this is my bowl

YOU WILL NEED

I enamel pudding bowl (the size depends on the size of your dog)
masking tape
clingfilm
blackboard paint or spray
chalk

1 Give your bowl a really good soapy scrub with a scouring pad to remove any surface dirt.

2 Mask off the bowl leaving the shape you wish to paint/spray and cover the rest of the bowl in clingfilm, taping down the edges.

3 Either spray or paint your bowl with several thin coats of paint (follow the manufacturer's specific instructions). Leave to dry.

4 Remove all the tape and clingfilm and tidy up any wayward paint edges with a sharp craft knife.

5 Scribble your pet's name in your best handwriting and wait for dinnertime.

nest

Make your dog as comfy as possible as they while away the hours in the land of nod, snoring peacefully, no doubt dreaming of chasing rabbits. They can snuggle up with a bone pillow and a knitted blanket in a rather fancy bed.

Make a special place for your dog to sleep by reusing an old drawer, suitcase, 'seen better days' basket or wine crate. By adding a lovely lining and popping in a comfy pillow, your dog's bed won't look out of place whatever room they choose to rest their weary head in. With everything removable and washable there will be no chance of nasty niffs or unwelcome bugs hiding, waiting to pounce.

a bed to sleep in

1 Before you begin, clean and make the base of your bed safe and free from any loose bits, sharp nails, hinges or anything else that could harm your dog.

2 Measure the base length and width, then add a 1cm seam allowance to each side. Cut a piece of fabric in this size.

3 Measure the depth of the box and add a 5cm seam allowance to the top edge and a 1cm seam allowance to all other edges. Cut a piece of fabric to this size.

4 Stitch the sides to the base (see below), leaving 1cm unstitched at each end of the seams.

5 Pin the corner seams together and stitch to create a box-shaped lining.

6 Neaten off the top edge with an overlock or zigzag stitch and then press over 5mm of fabric to the wrong side.

7 Lay one end of the elastic onto the other end and pin. Check to see if it fits around the top of the bed, making adjustments if necessary, then sew the ends together to make a flat join.

8 Stretch and pin the elastic evenly around the top edge of the lining and then, using the stretch stitch setting on your sewing machine, stitch with a wide zigzag, pulling the elastic taught as you sew.

9 Place the liner into the bed, folding the elastic edge over the top to keep it secure.

10 Pop in a comfy cushion (make one to size, see page 34) and place in the sunshine spot where your dog likes to take 40 winks.

All dogs like to snuggle down into a warm cosy blanket and dream of chasing rabbits. So why not knit them this super soft, fancy looking blanket to add to their bed, then the plump pile of sofa cushions will no longer call their name and illegal parking on the chair will be reduced to a minimum?

knitted dog blanket

Blanket

1 Cast on 129 stitches.

2 Knit in garter stitch (knit every row) for 40 rows.

3 Change colour and knit in garter stitch for 40 rows.

4 Repeat steps 1–2 until you have 5 blocks of colour. Cast off and sew in the ends.

Edging

1 Join the cream yarn into the first stitch on the right side of the blanket, on the bottom short edge.

2 1 chain and then double crochet into each stitch to the end. Turn and repeat for five rows.

3 1 chain, *work a double crochet into the next two stitches, slip stitch, 3 chain, slip stitch into next stitch to form a picot. Repeat from * to end. Bind off and sew in the ends.

4 Repeat edging steps 1–3 on the top edge.

Dogs love blankets nearly as much as they love bones

Give your dog a warm, snuggly place to sprawl out and sink into with this most comfy bed. The thermal duvet effect gives extra warmth, which will encourage more slumber time and a safe space for your dog to chill out and relax.

rest a weary head bed

1 Using either the bone or paw template on pages 41 and 52, trace onto the paper side of your bondaweb. Following the manufacturer's instructions, iron onto your piece of contrasting fabric.

2 Carefully cut out the design and place on the right side of one of your pieces of cover fabric. When you are happy with the placement, iron it onto the fabric.

3 Using a narrow zigzag stitch, machine-sew around the edges of your design.

4 Lay the second piece of fabric onto the first, right sides together, and pin or tack around the edges. Leave an opening at one end to enable you to insert the pillow. You could add a zip or envelope opening at this stage if you wish.

5 Leaving a 1cm seam, start sewing at one end of the opening and stitch around the edge until you reach the other end of the opening. Turn your cover over and repeat the above step following the previous seam line. This will give your cushion seams extra strength.

6 Clip the corners and then finish the seam with an overlock or narrow zigzag stitch, to prevent the edges from fraying when the pillow is washed.

7 Turn your cover to the right side and ease out the corners. Carefully steam the entire cover to shape.

8 Insert your duvet cushion, lining up the corners and making sure it is laying flat inside, then stitch the opening closed. Place in a draught-free corner and watch your dog slumber his day away.

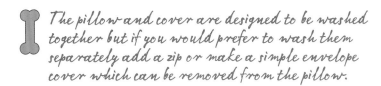

The pillow and cover are designed to be washed together but if you would prefer to wash them separately add a zip or make a simple envelope cover which can be removed from the pillow.

Make a smaller pillow by folding the duvet in half again and adjust your measurements accordingly.

If there is a pillow and a dog together in the same space then no matter how small the pillow you will always find the dog balancing on it trying to catch a few winks of sleep. So why not treat your dog to a pillow or two of their very own in this rather fun bone shape. Then there can be no doubt whose pillow belongs to whom....

bone pillow

1 Enlarge the bone template on page 41 on a photocopier to the size that you require for your pillow (remember to allow a 1cm seam allowance).

2 Cut out two bone shapes from your fabric and pin them together with the right sides facing.

3 Stitch around the edge of the bone, leaving the seam open where indicated on the template.

4 Trim the seam allowance and snip the seams on all the curves.

5 Turn the pillow to the right side out and stuff with polyester filling.

6 Sew the opening closed.

Best seat in the house....look where the dog is napping.

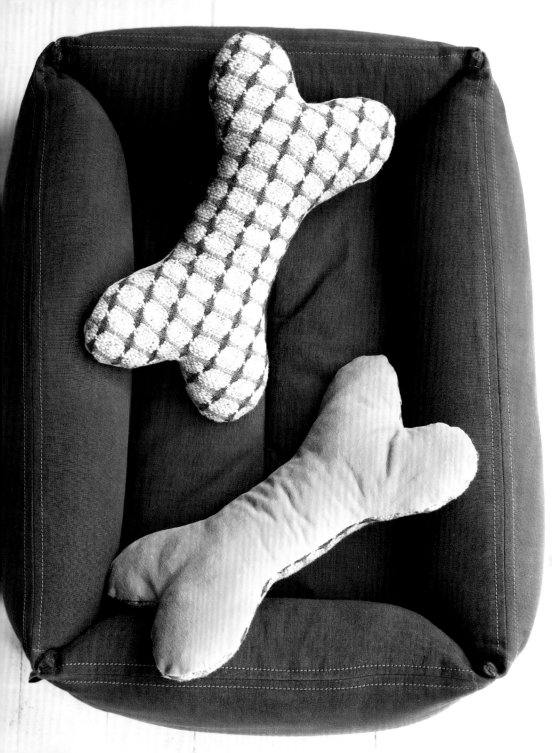

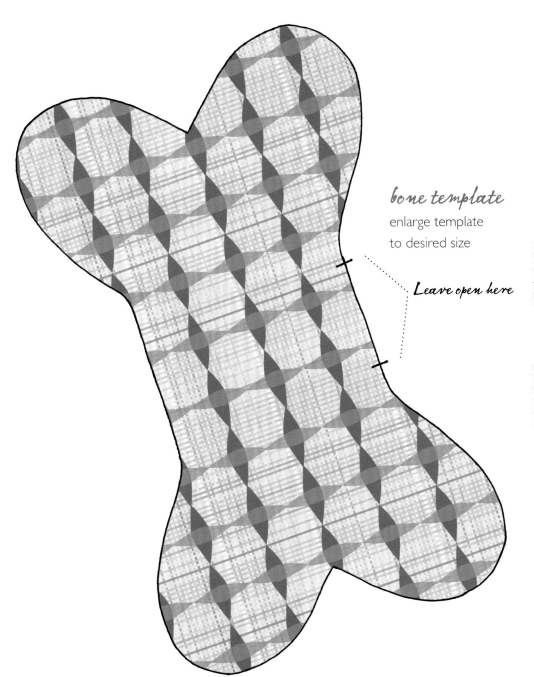

bone template
enlarge template
to desired size

Leave open here

Somehow owning a dog seems to come with all sorts of 'essential' paraphernalia. So to keep it all neat and tidy and in one place why not make this handy little wall shelf reserved for all things dog? Treats can sit up on top in the fancy containers you have made, while leads, dog towels and your Hanging Toy Basket (see page 70) can all be hung underneath.

handy wall shelf

YOU WILL NEED

2 pieces of wood approx. 30 x 9 x 2cm (an ideal project to reuse odds bit of wood)

wood glue

screws

medium-grain sandpaper

paint in your colour of choice – small sample pots are ideal for this but will need waxing afterwards to keep them in tip-top condition

2 small eyelet hooks*

2 screw-in door knobs

1 cup hook

1 Assemble your shelf by gluing along the long 2cm-thick edge and placing one piece of wood on top of the other in an L-shape, then screw them together. This will ensure you have a firm and sturdy shelf. Leave to dry for at least 24 hours.

2 Sand any rough edges and apply your first coat of paint. Repeat until you are happy with the finish. Apply wax if needed.

3 On the top edge of the shelf, mark in 5cm from each edge and screw in your eyelet hooks as close to the back edge of the wood as possible.

4 Mark on the shelf front where you want to place your knobs and cup hook and screw them in.

5 Fix your shelf to the wall by screwing through the eyelet hooks, then place all your doggie bits in their new home.

* You may wish to use a fixing more suitable for your wall.

Every dog needs a name banner to hang up high and proclaim to all and sundry that 'this is me' and this is my stuff. Hang this carefully stitched banner above their bed, over the Handy Wall Shelf (see page 42) where all their bits and bobs belong or in a special corner that gets the most sun and a carefully positioned cushion can be found.

'this is me' name banner

(see page 42)

YOU WILL NEED

various pieces of mismatched fabric

lace and ribbon trimmings

needle and black embroidery cotton

1 Cut a piece of fabric to the size you would like your banner (this one is 22 x 15cm) and neaten the edges with an overlock or zigzag stitch.

2 Pin onto the fabric the lace and trimmings until you are happy with the layout and then stitch them down.

3 Mark out your dog's name onto the banner and then with the embroidery cotton, and using a backstitch, carefully sew the name.

4 Add two pieces of folded tape or ribbon to each of the top corners and hang for all to see and know that this area is indeed a sacred dog space.

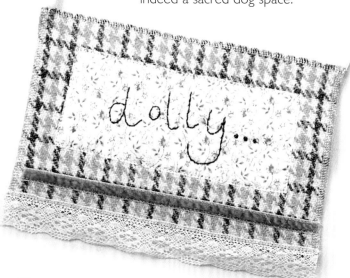

dolly...

Take a little piece of home with you to give your dog comfort when you are travelling far and wide. This roll-up bed is easy to keep in the boot of the car and will provide your dog with the perfect place to sleep when you are out and about exploring the countryside, staying with friends or off on your jolly holidays.

travelling dog bed

YOU WILL NEED

a strip of waxed cotton 5 x 100cm

65 x 95cm piece of waxed cotton

65 x 95cm fabric of your choice

62 x 92cm piece of cotton batting

tailor's chalk

a long darning needle and strong linen thread.

1 Make the travelling bed tie by folding the strip of waxed cotton in half, right sides together, and stitching down the length of the strip leaving a 1cm seam. Trim the seam allowance and turn the piece to the right side.

2 Fold the raw bottom edges of the tie to the inside and press. Top-stitch around all sides making sure you stitch close the two ends. Fold the tie in half.

3 Mark the centre point of the waxed cotton along the short edge and then lay the fold of the fabric tie in line with the edge of the fabric piece, strips facing towards the middle of the fabric. Baste stitch to keep the tie in place.

4 Pin the two fabric pieces right sides together, making sure your tie is sandwiched in between the two, and stitch a 1cm seam around the edges, leaving a 30cm gap at the end opposite the ties.

5 Snip the excess fabric at the corners, trim the seam allowances and then turn the cushion to the right side, easing out the corners.

6 Place the piece of batting inside the covers and smooth it out so that it lays flat inside, the corners are in corners and there are no lumps or bumps. Stitch the opening closed.

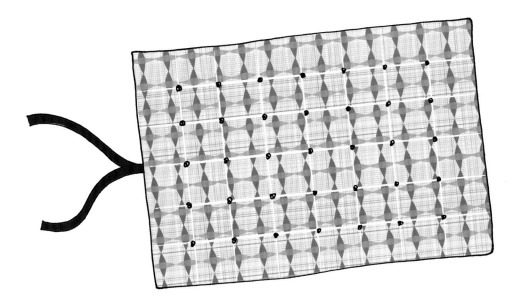

7 Using tailor's chalk, measure out evenly spaced lines across (8cm) down the length (12cm) to create a grid.

8 Using a strong thread and long needle, pass the needle through the point where the lines cross (see above). Bring the needle back through and tie the thread in a tight knot. Snip the thread. Repeat this until you have a grid of knots securing all the layers of the fabric, making a quilt-like effect.

9 Roll up the bed and secure with ties until your dog needs to rest its weary head.

Everyone deserves a treat at Christmas, including the critters in your home. Make this paw-shaped Christmas stocking and fill it with all kinds of handmade goodness, including toys, a fancy new collar and delicious things to munch and chew. Your dog will enjoy these treats much more than a bowl of turkey scraps. They'll charge through the pile of wrapping paper looking for general mischief, then snore their head off on the sofa… well, I hope they do.

Christmas stocking

YOU WILL NEED

50cm piece fake furry fabric

40 x 40cm felt or wool

40 x 40cm bondaweb

a strip of contrast fabric – twice the width of the top of the stocking + 2cm, x 14cm

a small piece of ribbon or tape to use as a hanger

1 Enlarge the stocking and paw templates on page 52 and use as a pattern to cut out the fabric. Pin the stocking template on the wrong side of the fur fabric and cut out the shape. Repeat for the other side.

2 Trace your paw shape onto the paper side of the bondaweb, then iron onto the wrong side of your felt or wool square. Cut out the paw shape and remove the backing paper. Using a warm iron and a cloth, press them to the right side of one of the stocking pieces.

3 Stitch around the edge of the paw shapes. You can use either a narrow zigzag stitch or a bit of free hand embroidery, depending on what you fancy.

4 Lay the two stocking pieces down, right sides facing, and pin around the edge. You may wish to tack the edge before you stitch to keep both pieces perfectly aligned. Stitch around the edge, then zigzag or overlock the seam to prevent it from fraying. Turn out to the right side.

5 Pin the hanging tape to the top edge of the stocking on the wrong side, near the side seam with the loop side facing downward.

6 Fold the strip of fabric in half and stitch the short side with a 1cm seam to create a band of fabric. Fold it in half lengthways with the wrong sides facing and press along the entire length to create a sharp fold.

7 Pin the band around the top of the stocking, with the right side of the band facing the wrong side of the stocking. Stitch together using a 1cm seam, ensuring you stitch the hanging loop between the band and stocking. Fold the band to the right side of the stocking and press.

To have better control of the fur fabric it is easier to cut each piece separately rather than together.

Christmas stocking

enlarge template 200%

play

When your dog isn't sleeping, eating or barking at something outside, they are playing. Make them a basket full of toys to throw and catch until they are ready to collapse in the corner with a heart full of joy.

Your dog will love chasing after this ball, stuffed full of fabric scraps. Its practical handle helps you to chuck it just a little bit further which may wear your dog out a little bit quicker. It can also be thrown in the washing machine if it gets too mucky… Hours of fun for you both.

chuck it fabric ball

YOU WILL NEED

a piece of fabric
20 x 50cm or 6 pieces
20 x 8cm if you would
like to use different
fabrics

2 pieces of cotton
twill tape 45cm long

small fabric scraps for
stuffing

strong thread and
needle

1 Using the ball template on page 58 cut out 6 pieces of fabric.

2 With right sides facing, pin and stitch 3 pieces of fabric together and then repeat with the other 3 pieces.

3 Place a piece of twill tape onto the opposite edges of one of the three stitched sections of the ball at the notch mark, making sure the tape is lying on the right side of the fabric, towards the centre of the ball. Stitch into place, sewing back and forth several times to attach the handle firmly.

4 With right sides facing and the twill tape inside the ball, sew the two remaining sides of the ball together, leaving an opening in one side to insert the stuffing.

5 Then fill the ball with small scraps of fabric and then stitch the opening closed with strong thread.

6 Hand stitch across each seam from the top to the bottom of the ball to give it extra strength.

7 Tie knots in your twill tape to form a handle with which to throw the ball.

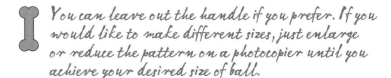

You can leave out the handle if you prefer. If you would like to make different sizes, just enlarge or reduce the pattern on a photocopier until you achieve your desired size of ball.

chuck it fabric ball

enlarge template 120%

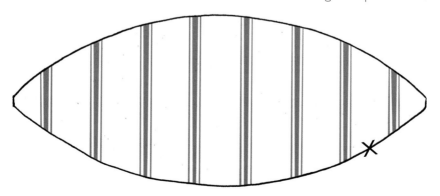

This toy was inspired by a rather wayward Jack Russell who likes to raid the recycling basket and spend his days dashing about the place with a plastic bottle in tow making a rather gleeful 'grrrrr' sound. To make a toy that will last just a little bit longer before it is discarded in the middle of the lawn, I added a cover that could be reused once the bottle inside had died a horrible chewed-up death. It also has the added bonus of preventing the plastic inside the cover being swallowed and harming your dog.

It has been designed for a regular 500ml plastic water bottle and you may need to tinker with the measurements to fit your usual brand.

grrrr toy

YOU WILL NEED

25 x 25cm non-fraying fabric for top of cover, such as fleece, felt or a piece of wool blanket

25 x 25cm sturdy fabric for bottom of cover (recycled jeans are excellent for this)

16cm piece of 1cm wide elastic

1 Neaten the edges of the bottom piece of your cover fabric with either an overlock or narrow zigzag stitch.

2 Lay the two pieces of fabric together with right sides facing and stitch a 1cm seam allowance along one side.

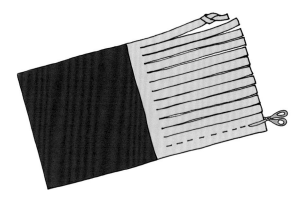

3 Lay the cover flat and cut the top fleece part of the cover into strips leaving about 2cm uncut at the base (see diagram above). Knot the top of each strip.

4 Fold your cover lengthways with right sides facing, and stitch the side seam of the bottom denim piece only. Leave the fleece seam open.

5 At the base, turn under a 1.5cm hem to create a channel for the elastic. Stitch the seam leaving an opening to thread the elastic through. Thread through the elastic and stitch the ends firmly together and then stitch the opening shut.

6 Sew a line of gathering stitches along the top of the uncut fleece just below the strips. Place your bottle into the cover and then gather the fleece together tightly and stitch through several times to secure the top of the cover. The bottle can be easily removed and replaced through the elastic opening at the base.

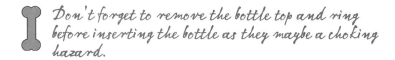

Don't forget to remove the bottle top and ring before inserting the bottle as they maybe a choking hazard.

If you are adding any embroidery or decoration to the lower part of the cover do this before you begin to assemble the pieces.

Does your dog like to catch their toys in mid-air, leaping from the ground to make that amazing save before the toy lands in a rather soggy patch of mud? If yes, then one or two of these frisbees are essential in your dog's toy box.

fetch frisbee

YOU WILL NEED

60m cotton yarn –
dishcloth yarn or
similar

needle and strong
linen thread

superglue

1 Measure 30 x 2m lengths of yarn. A quick and easy way to do this is to wind it round a 1m piece of wood or measuring rule and cut through the yarn at one end.

2 Lay the yarn lengths together and secure one end by winding a strong thread several times around the yarn and sewing a couple of stitches to secure.

3 Separate the yarn into 3 groups of 10 strands and then tightly plait until you have reached the end. Secure as before, by winding round strong thread. Don't break the thread.

4 Wrap the plait in a spiral around the end with the unbroken thread, stitching it together tightly as you go. Continue to wrap and stitch until you reach the end of the plait. Using several stitches make sure the end is well fastened in place.

5 Trim any excess yarn at both ends of your frisbee and gently squeeze a couple of drops of superglue onto the thread to seal it and stop it from fraying.

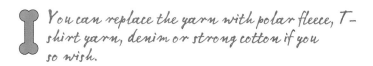

You can replace the yarn with polar fleece, T-shirt yarn, denim or strong cotton if you so wish.

Dogs always need another toy, this is the way it is and will always be. This toy is a great fabric stash buster and is a handy size and weight for a game of fetch, or catch, run off and chew, depending on how your dog likes to play.

throw-and-catch bone

YOU WILL NEED

2 pieces of fabric large enough to fit your template

polyester cushion filling

strong needle and thread

1 Using the bone template on page 41, cut out two bone shapes from your fabric and then pin them together, right sides facing.

2 Using a short stitch, sew around the edge of the bone leaving the seam open where indicated on the template. Turn the fabric open and sew the seam again following the previous line of stitches. This will make sure you have a really strong seam.

3 Trim the seam allowance and snip the seams on all the curves.

4 Turn the bone to the right side and stuff with polyester filling until really firm. Hand stitch the opening closed.

These jute strips are really quick and easy to crochet and will give your dog something to chew and throw about, plus with the jute string working like dental floss they will help keep their teeth and gums healthy.

chew it strips

YOU WILL NEED

ball of jute string
5mm crochet hook

1 Work 6 chain for your foundation row. Turn.

2 In the third chain from the hook, work a half treble crochet, then work 1 half treble crochet in the next 4 stitches. Turn.

3 Work 2 chain and then 1 half double crochet in each stitch until the end. Turn.

4 Repeat step 3 until you have 16 rows.

5 Bind off the last stitch and sew in the excess threads at each end so that they are unlikely to come undone when your dog is playing with the strips.

hanging toy basket

Dogs have a tendency to leave their toys all over the show, especially in places where you are most likely to step on them, risking life and limb as you try not to fall in a heap on the floor. Keep them all together safely out of the way with this nifty hanging basket, hung from a hook or door handle. Both you and your dog will know where their favourite squeaker is at all times.

YOU WILL NEED

130m ball Nutscene garden twine or similar garden jute twine

5.5mm crochet hook

1 Work 5 chain stitches and join the ring with a slip stitch into the first stitch.

2 Work 8 double crochet into the middle of the ring. Join with a slip stitch into the first stitch.

3 2 chain, work 1 half treble crochet in same stitch. Then 2 half treble crochet into the next 7 stitches. Join with a slip stich into the second chain stitch. (16 stitches)

4 2 chain, work *1 half treble crochet into next stitch, 2 half treble crochet into following stitch. Repeat from * to the end. Join with a slip stitch into the second chain stitch. (24 stitches)

5 2 chain, work *1 half treble crochet into the next 2 stitches, then 2 half treble crochet into following stitch. Repeat from * to end. Join with a slip stitch into the second chain stitch. (32 stitches)

6 2 chain, work *1 half treble crochet into next 3 stitches, then 2 half treble crochet into the following stitch. Repeat from *to end. Join with a slip stitch into the second chain stitch. (40 stitches)

7 2 chain, work *1 half treble crochet into next 4 stitches, then 2 half treble crochet into the following stitch. Repeat from * to end. Join with a slip stitch into the second chain stitch. (48 stitches)

8 2 chain, work 1 half treble crochet into each stitch to end. Join with a slip stitch into the second chain stitch. Repeat step 8 for 10 more rows.

9 1 chain, work double crochet into each stitch to end. Join with a slip stitch into the first chain.

10 Work a slip stitch into the next 3 double crochet and then work 20 chain. Count back 6 double crochet and attach the chain into the 6th double crochet space with a slip stitch.

11 Work 20 double crochet along the chain to form a hanging loop. Slip stitch into the last chain. Sew in the ends so the loop is secure.

Most dogs like nothing more than a mindless game of throw and fetch. Jute string is a cheap and natural material that makes a strong toy for your dog to enjoy but also has the benefit of cleaning your dog's teeth when they bite into it.

plaited fetch toy

YOU WILL NEED

I ball of jute string, cut into 30 x 45cm lengths

1 Lay the lengths of jute together, then tie one end into a firm knot, making sure there are no loose strands.

2 Separate the strings into three groups of ten.

3 Start to plait the string, taking care to keep it tight as you work. Once you have plaited approximately two-thirds, tie a tight knot at the bottom end. Again, making sure all the strings are pulled tight into the knot.

4 Throw your toy and then hope that your dog fetches it back…

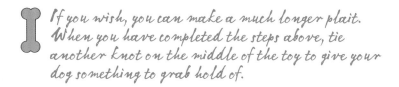

If you wish, you can make a much longer plait. When you have completed the steps above, tie another knot on the middle of the toy to give your dog something to grab hold of.

wear

A coat of fur is all a dog really needs, but a fancy collar, jaunty neck scarf or a stylish coat to keep out the chill wind are a few of the projects you can make to keep your dog looking their best each and every day.

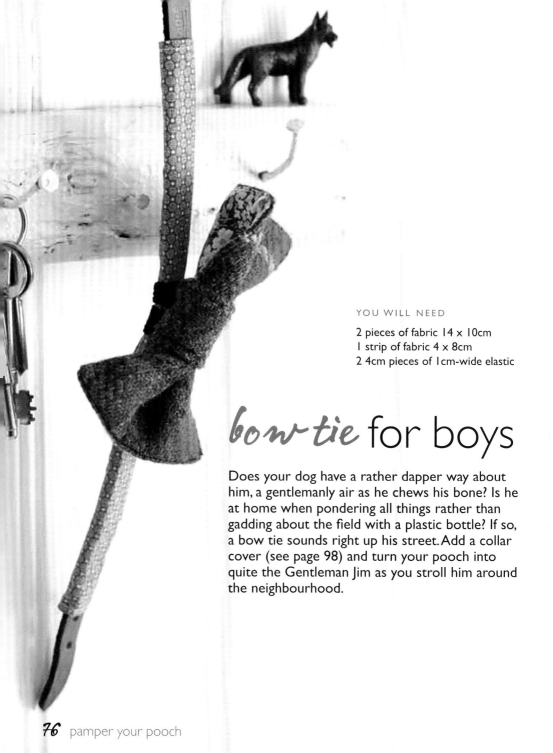

bow tie for boys

Does your dog have a rather dapper way about him, a gentlemanly air as he chews his bone? Is he at home when pondering all things rather than gadding about the field with a plastic bottle? If so, a bow tie sounds right up his street. Add a collar cover (see page 98) and turn your pooch into quite the Gentleman Jim as you stroll him around the neighbourhood.

1 With the right sides facing, pin the two 14 × 10cm pieces of fabric together, then stitch a 1cm seam allowance around the edge, leaving a small opening.

2 Trim the excess fabric from the corners and turn your rectangle of fabric right side out. Gently ease out the corners and seams and press into shape with an iron, then top stitch around the edge to close the opening.

3 Neaten the two long edges of the fabric strip by stitching a 5mm-wide hem on each side. Neaten the short ends with an over-locking or zigzag stitch to stop them fraying.

4 Wrap your strip around the middle of the rectangle to create a bow tie shape and hand stitch the ends in place.

5 Join the ends of each piece of elastic together, to form two loops, then stitch them both onto the back of the bow tie.

6 Slip onto your dog's collar at a jaunty angle for the world to see what a gentleman he truly is.

Ladies like to adorn themselves with pretty things, so why not make this sweet felt flower to give your pooch a bit of bling to wear on dull days. Choose bright, eye-catching colours and match with a Nifty Dog Collar Cover (see page 100) for a pooch who turns heads as she meanders along the street.

fancy flower for girls

YOU WILL NEED

2 sheets of different-coloured felt (approx. 30 x 30cm)

needle and matching thread

5cm of 2.5cm-wide elastic

1 Cut a 3 x 30cm strip from each sheet of felt.

2 Cut one piece in a scalloped shape and then the second strip in notches (see diagrams on page 80).

3 With the thread doubled, sew gathering stitches along the straight edge of the first piece of felt and tightly gather it into a flower shape, securing with several small stitches.

4 To make the centre of the flower, make several cuts along the length of second strip, ensuring you don't cut all the way through, then roll it up. Secure it with a few small stitches and then sew it to the middle of the felt flower. Don't skimp on the stitches, as it needs to be attached firmly.

5 Cut a circle from the remaining felt and firmly stitch this to the back of the flower to hold everything in place.

6 Fold the elastic in half, stitch the two ends together so it forms a loop and sew it on to the back of the flower.

7 The flower is now ready to slide onto your dog's collar.

No day is complete without wearing your favourite felted flowers...

fancy flower for girls
enlarge template 00%

There's nothing more jolly than seeing a dog sporting a rather dashing neckerchief, but they do have a tendency to cast them aside in the long grass while they are hunting for various small animals. To solve this problem, make your dog a handsome neckerchief that attaches to their collar – there will be no more glum faces or doggy sad eyes at a favourite scarf lost forever in the undergrowth.

jaunty neckerchief

YOU WILL NEED

2 squares of 22 x 22cm contrasting fabric

1 With the right sides facing, pin the fabric and stitch a 1cm seam around the edge, stitching across two of the corners (as shown below), leaving an opening to turn the fabric inside out.

2 Trim the corners of any excess fabric, then turn your fabric the right side out and gently ease out the corners and seams.

3 Press into shape with an iron, taking care that the seam at the opening is tucked inside. Pin to keep it in place.

4 Top stitch about 3mm from the edge around the entire piece; this will neatly close the open seam.

5 Fold the square in half diagonally, corner to furthest corner, and press.

6 Lay your dog's collar along the fold and mark the stitch line. Remember to allow a little extra for the depth of the collar (about 3–5mm).

7 Stitch along this line to create a channel to hold the collar.

8 Thread your collar through the channel and pop onto your dog.

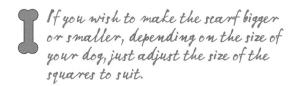

If you wish to make the scarf bigger or smaller, depending on the size of your dog, just adjust the size of the squares to suit.

When your day is grey there is nothing quite like the silent companionship of a dog.

Even the most robust of dogs feel the chill of a cold and blustery day. They may give you those 'let's stay by the fire' eyes as you grab your coat and their lead. Why not give them a little extra warmth and keep the wind at bay by crocheting this rather lovely cowl? Team it with the Dandy Dog Coat on page 92 and your pooch will be ready to walk in all weather.

keep warm crochet cowl

YOU WILL NEED

Aran-weight yarn in 2 colours
5mm crochet hook

Main Cowl

1 Measure around the widest part of your dog's neck and add 2cm (measurement A).

2 Measure from the base of the neck at the shoulders to just below the ears (measurement B).

3 Work a multiple of 3 chain for your foundation row until it reaches measurement A.

4 Slip stitch into the first chain to create a ring.

5 Work 3 chain (the first treble), then work 2 treble crochet into the same stitch.

6 Skip a 2 chain.

7 Work 3 treble crochet in the next chain stitch and repeat to the end of the row.

8 Slip stitch into the third chain.

9 Work 3 chain (the first treble), then in each group of 3 trebles, work *1 treble in space between 1 and 2 trebles, 1 chain, 1 treble in the space between trebles 2 and 3. Repeat from * to the last group of 3 treble crochet, then work 1 treble, 1 chain and slip stitch into the third chain.

10 Work 3 chain, 3 treble crochet into each 1 chain space until the last space, then work 2 trebles and slip stitch into the third chain.

11 Work steps 9 and 10 until the cowl reaches measurement B, then sew in the ends.

Top edge

1 Join the yarn into any space on the top edge. Work 1 double crochet into each stitch until the end.

2 Slip stitch into the first double crochet and sew in the ends.

Bottom edge

1 Join the yarn into any space on the bottom edge. Work 1 double crochet into each stitch until the end, then slip stitch into the first double crochet.

2 Work 1 chain, then double crochet into each stitch. Slip stitch into the first double crochet.

3 Work *1 slip stitch into the next 2 stitches, slip stitch, 3 chain, slip stitch into the next stitch, making a picot, then repeat from * to the end and sew in the ends.

As every dog owner knows, bathing a dog can be a rather soggy experience. Trying to negotiate wrapping them in a towel while lifting them from the bath often leads to disaster and the dog's determination to get away and have a good shake is second to none. By adapting a bath sheet this task is made a breeze and a dry bathroom is an added bonus.

bath-day towel

YOU WILL NEED

1 large bath sheet (100 x 150cm)

5m bias binding

scraps of contrast fabric or felt for a paw-print motif, optional

1 Begin by cutting a 1 x 1m square from your towel. Save the excess piece to use later.

2 Lay the towel out flat and then from one corner measure and mark 20cm along. Repeat on the opposite side. Draw a line across and cut along it to remove the corner piece of fabric. Place to one side.

3 Cut a square 50 x 50cm from the excess fabric, then cut in half to make two triangles.

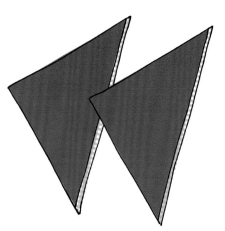

4 Stitch bias binding across the diagonal to seal the raw seam.

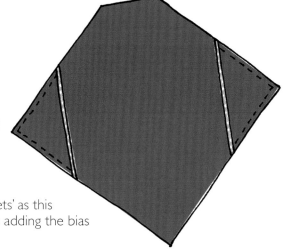

5 With the flat part of the main towel at the top, pin the two triangle pieces to opposite corners with the bias binding facing the middle.

6 Tack the outside seams of the 'pockets' as this will make stitching easier when you are adding the bias tape.

7 Stitch bias binding around the entire edge of the towel, making sure you secure all layers at the pocket corners.

8 To make the neck strap (which goes over your head, not the dog's!) cut a 50cm piece of bias binding and fold it in half, then stitch together along the long side. Fold over each end into the inside to neaten.

9 Attach one end of your strap to the towel and stitch on. Before you stitch the other side, pin the strap and try it on around your head and make adjustments in the length if necessary.

10 To add a paw print motif, cut out the shape from some contrasting fabric and then pin onto your towel. Using a narrow zigzag stitch on your sewing machine, stitch around the outside edges to secure your shape to the towel.

11 Immediately give your dog a bath to give your towel a whirl.

There are days when your dog needs a little help keeping cosy and snug when venturing out of the house. This toasty overcoat will keep your pooch warm and dry on the windiest and wettest of days, with the added bonus of helping to minimize the amount of mess and debris that your dog will collect in their coat and sneak back into the house. Team it with the crochet cowl (see page 83) and your dog will be sorted whatever the weather.

dandy dog coat

YOU WILL NEED

paper for template

50cm waxed cotton or similar waterproof fabric (you may need more if you have a large dog)

50cm polar fleece fabric

15cm sew-on Velcro, or other hook and loop fastener

Before you begin, you will need to take the following measurements from your dog. Have a few treats on hand to get them to stand still.

A measure from the base of the neck (just below collar) to the tail, then add 2cm.
B measure around the ribcage behind the front legs. Half this measurement, then add 5cm.
C measure around the front of the chest from behind the front legs. Half this measurement, then add 2cm.
D measure around the neck just below where the collar sits, then divide by three.

1 Once you have all your measurements, make a paper template, starting by drawing a rectangle using measurements A and B on a large folded piece of paper.

2 At the bottom right hand corner, extend the line by measurement C, then draw a line up 10cm (see i on page 94).

3 Divide measurement D in half and mark this point from top right corner (see ii on page 94).

4 Join point (i) and (ii) with a gentle curve, then round off the bottom left corner and the front strap corners. Cut an 8 x 25cm paper belly strap.

5 Try your paper pattern on your dog and attach the belly strap just behind the front legs, then adjust the length for a comfy fit.

6 When you are happy with the fit, cut two of each of your patterns (including the belly strap): one set from the waterproof fabric and one set from the polar fleece.

7 With the right sides facing, pin your fabric. If you are using waxed cotton, pin in the seam allowance and remove the pins as you sew so you don't damage the fabric.

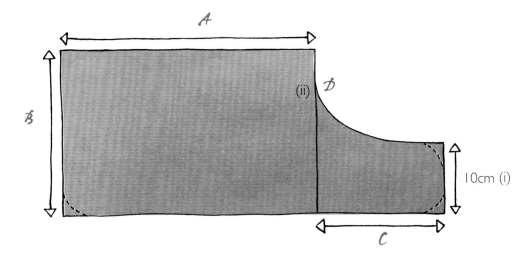

A

B

(ii) D

10cm (i)

C

8 Stitch around the edge, leaving an opening on the back edge to allow you to turn the coat.

9 Trim the fabric at the curves and turn it right side out, carefully easing out the seams. Press gently using an iron. If the fabric is waxed cotton, use a piece of greaseproof paper to protect your iron.

10 Sew two lines of top stitch, the first close to the edge to close the opening, and then another about 5mm from the first.

11 Cut 10cm of Velcro and stitch it onto the chest straps.

12 Repeat steps 7–12 for the belly strap.

13 Pin the belly strap to one side of the coat and stitch using a double line of stitch to make sure it stays put.

14 On the opposite end of the belly strap, stitch one side of your Velcro. Try the coat on your dog and mark on where to stitch the other piece of Velcro, making sure that it is a snug fit but not so tight that it restricts movement. Then, stitch the second piece of Velcro onto the coat.

The paper template can be used to try the coat out for size on your dog and make adjustments before you cut your fabric. Remember, it allows for seams so it will be a little bigger than the finished coat.

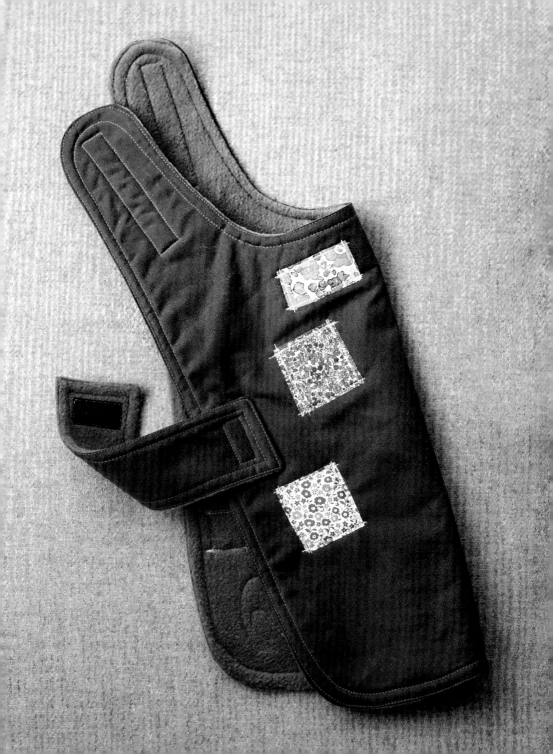

A wonderful long walk with your dog is often blighted by the subsequent 'muddy paw mess' that follows at home as they whip past you at the last minute to run riot on your floors or carpet. This muddy paw towel is quick and easy to use and should cut down on the mess unleashed on your floors.

muddy paw towel

YOU WILL NEED

1 bath towel
3m 2cm-wide bias binding tape
small piece of ribbon or tape
small fabric pieces for paw print, optional

1 Begin by cutting a 25 x 110cm rectangle from the bath towel (adjust length if your towel comes up shorter).

2 Cut two 25 x 30cm pocket pieces from the remaining bath towel and place to one side.

3 Fold the rectangle in half lengthwise and mark and round off the corners. You may want to make a paper template for the rounded corners to make both sides equal.

4 On one short edge of the pocket piece, bind the raw edge with bias tape. Repeat for the second piece. If you are adding a paw print design, stitch it onto the pocket now (instructions as for bath towel, see page 88).

5 Pin the pocket pieces to each end of the rectangle and round off the corners to match. Tack them down, as this will make it easier when adding the bias tape.

6 Sew bias binding tape around the edges, ensuring that both layers are covered at the pocket ends.

7 Sew the ribbon or tape about half way along the rectangle, so you can hang the towel up in easy reach of the door.

8 To use the towel, place your hands into the pockets and rub your dog's paws to remove the mud – and save yourself a whole lot of scrubbing or mopping.

crochet handle
for dull dog leads

Dog leads are not the most attractive things for your dog to wear. They are practical, they keep your dog safe in sticky situations that he or she may stumble into on your daily walk, but – let's face it – they are dull. This colourful handle cover brightens up the dullest of dog leads and makes it a little more comfortable for your hands when faced with unruly pulling.

YOU WILL NEED

double knit yarn in various colours
4mm crochet hook
wool needle

1 Work 10 chain for your foundation row (check this will fit round your lead handle and add or minus stitches accordingly. Turn.

2 Chain 2 stitches, then 1 double crochet into each stitch. Turn and repeat for the following rows.

3 Work as many rows in each colour as you fancy and keep checking the length around the handle as you work. When changing to a new shade, sew in the ends, leaving one long piece of yarn. You will use this to join the handle around the lead.

4 When you have reached your desired length, cast off, then wrap the cover around the handle of your lead, joining the long edges facing the middle.

5 Carefully stitch the edges together using the yarn tails left from each colour, then sew in the ends and take your dog out for a walk.

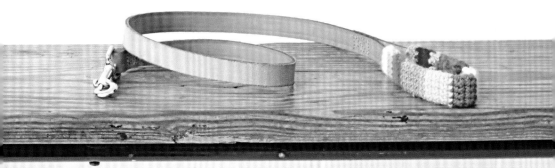

Dog collars can be tricky things to keep clean and, as they are worn all the time, they have a tendency to niff a bit. These collar covers add a ditsy jolly print or two to your dog's wardrobe and have the added bonus that they can be removed and popped into the washing machine to keep your pooch's collar smelling A-okay.

nifty dog collar covers

YOU WILL NEED

paper for template
strip of fabric **2.5 times wider than your** dog's collar

1 Measure from the 'D' ring to the hole that you use to fasten the collar and add 2cm.

2 Measure the width of the collar, double it, then add 1.5cm.

3 Make yourself a paper template using the collar measurements, pin it to the fabric and cut out the pattern.

4 Turn over a 1cm seam on either end with the wrong sides facing. Press it with an iron and stitch along 5mm from the edge.

5 With the right sides facing, fold the piece of fabric in half and pin it in place. Stitch a 1cm seam along the length of the fabric. Overlock or trim 5mm from the seam allowance, then use a narrow zigzag stitch to finish the seam.

6 Turn out to the right side using a loop turner or good old safety pin and slip onto the collar, then gently iron the seam open, taking care with the heat setting, especially if you have a leather collar.

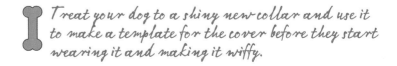

Treat your dog to a shiny new collar and use it to make a template for the cover before they start wearing it and making it wiffy.

Stockists

Don't just limit yourself to pet shops when buying bits and bobs for your dog. Keep an eye out in charity shops as many of them have a special 'dog' blanket and towel box in which many a treasure can be found. Always be on the look out for old woollens, enamel bowls and tins as you can never have enough when it comes to pets of a doggy nature.

Eat

Cutters
If a bone-shaped cookie cutter takes
your fancy and you can't find one
anywhere, try
www.cakescookiesandcraftsshop.co.uk

Plastic dog food lids
www.petsathome.co.uk

Play

Jute string
Nutscene's jute string is the only string
that I have been able to use to crochet,
plus they have the most fab colours
www.nutscene.com

Nest

Aran yarn
Woolcraft, Sirdar and James C Brett all
do excellent yarns that will wash and
wash no matter how much your dog
tries to scruff it up. Also try your local
independent wool shop or search for
online stockists.
www.deramores.com

Dog-friendly fabrics
Most of the fabric used in this book can
be found at your local fabric shop or
market stall. For online fabric Abakhan
have a great range of fur and fleece
fabric.
www.abakhan.co.uk

Wear

Waxed fabric
This is pretty much impossible to find,
except on good old eBay. Fab Crafts
UK stocks great quality fabric for a most
sensible price.
www. stores.ebay.co.uk/Fab-Crafts-UK

Index

Acknowledgements

This book is dedicated to all the dogs that have crossed my path over the years, but especially Paddy the Poodle, who patiently allowed my sister and I to dress him up for hours on end in various ridiculous outfits. To Stanley, who has been measured, modelled and made to sit for ages whilst I road tested the patterns, and rudely removed from cushions and blankets when he tried to sneak in a quick nap.

To Judith, for coming up with this crazy idea of writing the book; it has been such fun and I'm sorry for laughing at you when you suggested it. To Claire, for sorting out all the bits and bobs and everyone else at Kyle Books who beaver on behind the scenes making books happen.

To Mark, for the great design, and especially to Dudley, Casper and Miss Mollie, who stole a little bit of my heart forever.

To Kate & Polly and your doggy pals for fab photos and styling. I am more than a little bit chuffed.

A big thank you to Mungo and Maud, Purple Bone, Holly and Lil and Verve-London for lending us all sorts of doggy paraphernalia to get the great shots throughout the book.

And last but not least to all you dog owners out there who are feeling a little crafty. Making something for you dog might not be the quickest and easiest path, considering that there is every possibility that it may be destroyed in 10 seconds flat but you will enjoy every step of the process and your heart will shine when you see them snuggled up on the bed you made or proudly strutting their fancy collar in the park.

The models

Dudley

Zippy

Peggy

Digby

Miss Mollie

Badger

Raj

Stanley

Bella

Sweep

Checky

Casper

Moses

First published in Great Britain in 2014 by
Kyle Books, an imprint of Kyle Cathie Ltd.
192–198 Vauxhall Bridge Road
London SW1V 1DX
general.enquiries@kylebooks.com
www.kylebooks.com

Printer line 10 9 8 7 6 5 4 3 2 1

ISBN 978 0 85783 260 3

Project Editor: Judith Hannam
Designer: Mark Latter
Photographer: Kate Whitaker
Prop Stylist: Polly Webb-Wilson
Production: Nic Jones, Gemma John

A Cataloguing in Publication record for this title is available from the British Library.

Colour reproduction by ALTA London
Printed and bound in China by C&C Offset Printing Co., Ltd.

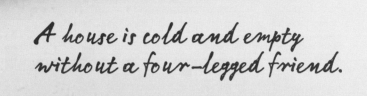

A house is cold and empty without a four-legged friend.

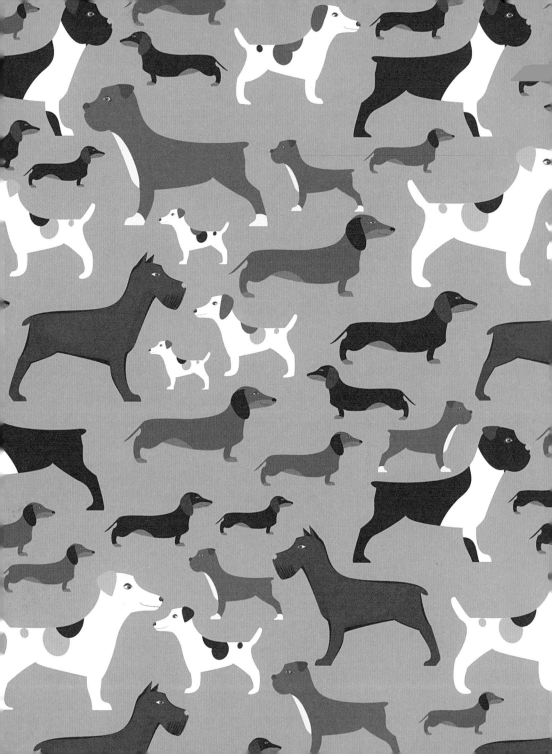